FRANCIS FRITH'S

LYME REGIS

PHOTOGRAPHIC MEMORIES

Prolific writer and countryside campaigner **RODNEY LEGG** has become the doyen of Dorset historians. Born in Bournemouth in 1947, as a teenager he walked every right of way in the county. Having founded both Tyneham Action Group and the Dorset County Magazine in 1968, he has gone on to write some 80 books. They range from comprehensive studies such as 'Dorset's War Diary' and 'Dorset Families' to local titles including 'The Book of Lyme Regis', 'The Book of Bridport' and 'Tyneham'; he has also written a biographical guide, 'Dorset's Hardy Country'. His personal crusades across a quarter of a century eventually succeeded in having Hardy's home at Max Gate opened to the public, and ensured the preservation of Fort Henry overlooking Studland Bay. Nationally he remains active in the environment movement. Since 1989 he has been chairman of the Open Spaces Society and a member of the ruling council of the National Trust.

FRANCIS FRITH'S
PHOTOGRAPHIC MEMORIES

LYME REGIS

PHOTOGRAPHIC MEMORIES

RODNEY LEGG

First published in the United Kingdom in 2005 by
The Francis Frith Collection®

Hardback edition 2005 ISBN 1-84589-016-7

Paperback edition 2005 ISBN 1-85937-956-6

British Library Cataloguing in Publication Data

Lyme Regis - Photographic Memories
Rodney Legg

The Francis Frith Collection
Frith's Barn, Teffont,
Salisbury, Wiltshire SP3 5QP
Tel: +44 (0) 1722 716 376
Email: info@francisfrith.co.uk
www.francisfrith.co.uk

Printed and bound in Great Britain

Front Cover: **LYME REGIS**, *Broad Street 1909* 61627t
Frontispiece: **LYME REGIS**, *The Cobb 1906* 54528

*The colour-tinting is for illustrative purposes only, and is not intended
to be historically accurate*

Aerial photographs reproduced under licence from
Simmons Aerofilms Limited.
Historical Ordnance Survey maps reproduced under licence from
Homecheck.co.uk

Every attempt has been made to contact copyright holders of
illustrative material. We will be happy to give full acknowledgement
in future editions for any items not credited. Any information
should be directed to The Francis Frith Collection.

AS WITH ANY HISTORICAL DATABASE THE FRITH ARCHIVE IS
CONSTANTLY BEING CORRECTED AND IMPROVED AND THE
PUBLISHERS WOULD WELCOME INFORMATION ON OMISSIONS OR
INACCURACIES

CONTENTS

FRANCIS FRITH
VICTORIAN PIONEER

FRANCIS FRITH, founder of the world-famous photographic archive, was a complex and multi-talented man. A devout Quaker and a highly successful Victorian businessman, he was philosophical by nature and pioneering in outlook.

By 1855 he had already established a wholesale grocery business in Liverpool, and sold it for the astonishing sum of £200,000, which is the equivalent today of over £15,000,000. Now a very rich man, he was able to indulge his passion for travel. As a child he had pored over travel books written by early explorers, and his fancy and imagination had been stirred by family holidays to the sublime mountain regions of Wales and Scotland. 'What lands of spirit-stirring and enriching scenes and places!' he had written. He was to return to these scenes of grandeur in later years to 'recapture the thousands of vivid and tender memories', but with a different purpose. Now in his thirties, and captivated by the new science of photography, Frith set out on a series of pioneering journeys up the Nile and to the Near East that occupied him from 1856 until 1860.

INTRIGUE AND EXPLORATION

These far-flung journeys were packed with intrigue and adventure. In his life story, written when he was sixty-three, Frith tells of being held captive by bandits, and of fighting 'an awful midnight battle to the very point of surrender with a deadly pack of hungry, wild dogs'. Wearing flowing Arab costume, Frith arrived at Akaba by camel sixty years before Lawrence of Arabia, where he encountered 'desert princes and rival sheikhs, blazing with jewel-hilted swords'.

He was the first photographer to venture beyond the sixth cataract of the Nile. Africa was still the mysterious 'Dark Continent', and Stanley and Livingstone's historic meeting was a decade into the future. The conditions for picture taking confound belief. He laboured for hours in his wicker dark-room in the sweltering heat of the desert, while the volatile chemicals fizzed dangerously in their trays. Back in London he exhibited his photographs and was 'rapturously cheered' by members of the Royal Society. His reputation as a photographer was made overnight.

VENTURE OF A LIFE-TIME

Characteristically, Frith quickly spotted the opportunity to create a new business as a specialist publisher of photographs. He lived in an era of immense and sometimes violent change.

For the poor in the early part of Victoria's reign work was exhausting and the hours long, and people had precious little free time to enjoy themselves. Most had no transport other than a cart or gig at their disposal, and rarely travelled far beyond the boundaries of their own town or village. However, by the 1870s the railways had threaded their way across the country, and Bank Holidays and half-day Saturdays had been made obligatory by Act of Parliament. All of a sudden the working man and his family were able to enjoy days out and see a little more of the world.

With typical business acumen, Francis Frith foresaw that these new tourists would enjoy having souvenirs to commemorate their days out. In 1860 he married Mary Ann Rosling and set out on a new career: his aim was to photograph every city, town and village in Britain. For the next thirty years he travelled the country by train and by pony and trap, producing fine photographs of seaside resorts and beauty spots that were keenly bought by millions of Victorians. These prints were painstakingly pasted into family albums and pored over during the dark nights of winter, rekindling precious memories of summer excursions.

THE RISE OF FRITH & CO

Frith's studio was soon supplying retail shops all over the country. To meet the demand he gathered about him a small team of photographers, and published the work of independent artist-photographers of the calibre of Roger Fenton and Francis Bedford. In order to gain some understanding of the scale of Frith's business one only has to look at the catalogue issued by Frith & Co in 1886: it runs to some 670 pages, listing not only many thousands of views of the British Isles but also many photographs of most European countries, and China, Japan, the USA and Canada - note the sample page shown on page 9 from the hand-written Frith & Co ledgers recording the pictures. By 1890 Frith had created the greatest specialist photographic publishing company in the world, with over 2,000 sales outlets - more than the combined number that Boots and WH Smith have today! The picture on the next page shows the Frith & Co display board at Ingleton in the Yorkshire Dales (left of window). Beautifully constructed with a mahogany frame and gilt inserts, it could display up to a dozen local scenes.

POSTCARD BONANZA

The ever-popular holiday postcard we know today took many years to develop. In 1870 the Post Office issued the first plain cards, with a pre-printed stamp on one face. In 1894 they allowed other publishers' cards to be sent through the mail with an attached adhesive halfpenny stamp. Demand grew rapidly, and in 1895 a new size of postcard was permitted called the court card, but there was little room for illustration. In 1899, a year after Frith's death, a new card measuring 5.5 x 3.5 inches became the standard format, but it was not until 1902 that the divided back came into being, so that the address and message could be on one face and a full-size illustration on the other. Frith & Co were in the vanguard of postcard development: Frith's sons Eustace and Cyril continued their father's monumental task, expanding the number of views offered to the public and recording more and more places in Britain, as the coasts and countryside were opened up to mass travel.

Francis Frith had died in 1898 at his villa in Cannes, his great project still growing. The archive he created continued in business for another seventy years. By 1970 it contained over a third of a million pictures showing 7,000 British towns and villages.

FRANCIS FRITH'S LEGACY

Frith's legacy to us today is of immense significance and value, for the magnificent archive of evocative photographs he created provides a unique record of change in the cities, towns and villages throughout Britain over a century and more. Frith and his fellow studio photographers revisited locations many times down the years to update their views, compiling for us an enthralling and colourful pageant of British life and character.

We are fortunate that Frith was dedicated to recording the minutiae of everyday life, for it is this sheer wealth of visual data, the painstaking chronicle of changes in dress, transport, street layouts, buildings, housing, engineering and landscape that captivates us so much today. His remarkable images offer us a powerful link with the past and with the lives of our ancestors.

THE VALUE OF THE ARCHIVE TODAY

Computers have now made it possible for Frith's many thousands of images to be accessed almost instantly. Frith's images are increasingly used as visual resources, by social historians, by researchers into genealogy and ancestry, by architects and town planners, and by teachers involved in local history projects.

In addition, the archive offers every one of us an opportunity to examine the places where we and our families have lived and worked down the years. Highly successful in Frith's own era, the archive is now, a century and more on, entering a new phase of popularity. Historians consider the Francis Frith Collection to be of prime national importance. It is the only archive of its kind remaining in private ownership. Francis Frith's archive is now housed in an historic timber barn in the beautiful village of Teffont in Wiltshire. Its founder would not recognize the archive office as it is today. In place of the many thousands of dusty boxes containing glass plate negatives and an all-pervading odour of photographic chemicals, there are now ranks of computer screens. He would be amazed to watch his images travelling round the world at unimaginable speeds through internet lines.

The archive's future is both bright and exciting. Francis Frith, with his unshakeable belief in making photographs available to the greatest number of people, would undoubtedly approve of what is being done today with his lifetime's work. His photographs depicting our shared past are now bringing pleasure and enlightenment to millions around the world a century and more after his death.

LYME REGIS
AN INTRODUCTION

THIS COLLECTION is graced by six of the best images in the whole of the Frith archive. One I shall describe as that Meryl Streep moment: it captures a wave crashing against the outer breakwater of the Cobb, a precursor of the scene that starred on the film poster for 'The French Lieutenant's Woman' by Lyme author John Fowles. The combination of Lyme Regis and the camera won the American actress a BAFTA award for that performance in 1981. Jane Austen did something similar in words to immortalise Granny's Teeth at the Cobb as the place where Louisa Musgrove fell in 'Persuasion'. There, a century later, Frith's photographer found two little girls for an exquisite Edwardian period piece.

Famous fictional personages continue to patronise Lyme. Inspector Morse rounded off the 20th-century batch by staying in Room 23 at The Bay Hotel, and enthused over the panoramic view from Marine Parade, as the author Colin Dexter confirmed when he unveiled a plaque in 2003.

The third of my favourite images shows

LYME REGIS, *From the West 1890* 27344

Samuel Govier in his forge, on the site of Woolworths in Broad Street, where the artist James Abbott McNeill Whistler found 'The Master Smith' of Lyme Regis. Whister's canvas hangs in the Boston Museum. Frith's photograph is a worthy companion, and captures the fading glory of this Regency spa.

The fourth and fifth of my favourites, the Lynch Walk at its rustic best in 1892 and prim and proper Sherborne Lane in 1907, are perfectly composed masterpieces from the heyday of Victorian and Edwardian photographic studies. I have original postcards of several of these, which were sent to my own family and friends or bought as souvenirs.

The sixth is the missing link between Lyme's past and the present. The Fossil Depot in Bridge Street, fronting what was then the oldest collection of buildings in the town, was photographed a decade before its demolition. This, the saddest of losses during the 20th century, removed two of the town's most poignant and picturesque corners. The other was at Jericho, beside the River Lim, where Baptist settlers squatted in thatched hovels.

It is impossible now to visit Lyme and its Jurassic coast without realising that you have ventured into the heart of a World Heritage Site. Fossils appear in the rocks and on the beach. I am drawn to the view of rock pools beneath the Bay Hotel, seen at the time of an incredibly low tide in 1930, and the picture of Cannington Viaduct, which is an engineering achievement in concrete on an unprecedented scale for these parts. It dominates the countryside across the border where Devon meets Dorset. Here the ruling family was that of the Peeks at Rousdon.

The Peeks were London tea and spice importers. The first baronet, Sir Henry William Peek (1825-98), created the 1,100-acre estate and built its great house in the Victorian Gothic style (see photograph 46050 on page 14). The second baronet, Sir Cuthbert Edgar Peek (1855-1901), a notable meteorologist and astronomer, established Rousdon Observatory. The third baronet, Captain Sir Wilfrid Peek (1884-1927) of the 1st Royal Devon Yeomanry, married Edwine Warner from St Louis in 1913, and their son, Sir Francis Peek (1915-96) went off to the Bahamas, where he was aide-de-camp to the governor, and then retired to Spain.

Below, the landscape of the Undercliff was becoming an almost impenetrable scrub, with a single oasis of civilisation provided by Miss Annie Gapper from her home in the Chasm on Dowlands Landslip into the 1930s (see photograph 45263, page 13). There was a lifebelt above the front door of the eastern semi-detached thatched cottage, and here her mother prepared the cakes and tea for her daughter to serve to visitors beside the trellis of rose bushes in the south-facing garden.

Lyme's scenery continues to be shaped by active geology, and can claim the biggest mud-flows in Europe. Major earth movements have moved eastwards along the coast. First there were multiple peaks of a massive slippage between Branscombe and Beer Head in the winter of 1789. What was described as 'the subsidence of the land and elevation of the bottom of the sea' at Dowlands took place on Boxing Day in 1839. There a cottage was left in the picturesque isolation of a chasm three-quarters of a mile long and 400 feet wide. Nearby Whitlands slipped on 3 February 1840. Rousdon trembled again on 3 October 1901.

East of Lyme, from the Spittles below Timber Hill to the Devil's Bellows at Charmouth, Black Ven now forms a National Trust nature reserve. The area self-combusted - through the action of water on iron pyrites and bituminous shale - in August 1751. Fires resumed several times later that century, and then erupted again on 19 January 1908. This 'Lyme Volcano' continued to burn until June, and resumed smouldering on two subsequent occasions.

This instability claimed the Old Lyme Road in the 1920s. The ground moved again in 1938, 1957-58, and 1969-70. Eye-witness accounts from 1958 include a vivid description of trees that marched across the skyline as they headed for oblivion on a mountain of debris which changed the coastline with a great bulge that pushed out to sea. Langmoor Gardens, above the Cobb, were extended over a development site after this caused a landslip in 1962; the collateral damage was the need for new retaining walls. Cliff Cottage lurched Pisa-like on 6 April 1963, but was later righted. An alternative route from Lyme to Charmouth,

via Old Road Hill and Foxley Ridge, subsided into the undercliff during the 1969 slippages. Sections of the coastal path continue to slip seawards with annoying regularity. Many have been diverted.

These landslips have created Lyme's uniquely jumbled scenery. They have been the mechanism that brought dinosaurs and other fossils into captivity in museums across Britain and Europe, and triggered the scientific study of life on earth. Both in quantity and quality they would impress the pioneer palaeontologist Mary Anning.

Sometimes, after two centuries of serious study, there are still some surprises. One such, among a multitude of ichthyosaur specimens, was a rare maritime reptile excavated on the beach near Golden Cap in November 2004. Dr Paul Davies of the National History Museum announced that it was only the second to be uncovered from the lower Pliensbachian stage of the Jurassic period. Though they looked much like present-day dolphins, ichthyosaurs were marine reptiles, which lived from 220 to 65 million years ago. As this book went to print, the ichthyosaur was going back home on a spring vacation with the Fossil Roadshow, which visited Lyme Regis in April 2005.

LANDSCAPE

ROUSDON, *Landslip Cottage 1900* 45263

The Gapper family cottage on Dowlands Landslip was approached from the coast path, after having been detached from the hamlet above to which it formerly belonged. The crags and chasm to the north date from December 1839. On Christmas Day, creaks and rumbles were heard, likened to thunder by farm workers and artillery fire by the veterans of Waterloo. The ground then shuddered and collapsed on Boxing Day. Only the remains of ivy-clad walls now survive in the heart of Undercliff National Nature Reserve, which is managed by English Nature.

▼ **ROUSDON,** *Rousdon House 1900* 46050

The Peek mansion at Rousdon was built by spice importer Sir Henry William Peek in 1877. Built on a massive plinth, with balustrades above and cellars below, the high-Gothic lines of Rousdon House rise above lawns which slope away towards the Undercliff. A museum was established here by Sir Henry's successor, the second baronet Sir Cuthbert Edgar Peek, principally for meteorological information and memorabilia. He travelled to Australia to measure and monitor an eclipse. The Peeks employed a small army of workers at Rousdon, of whom thirteen were killed in the First World War. In 1937, All Hallows School moved from Honiton to Rousdon House, which remained in educational use until 1997.

▶ **ROUSDON**

The Church 1900 46054

Built in the 1870s by Sir Herbert William Peek, St Pancras's Church at Rousdon replaced a small thatched Norman building. Kathleen Marian Peek, who died in 1952, was the last member of the family to be buried here. The church was declared redundant by an order in council signed by the Queen on 24 May 1972, and transferred to the governors of All Hallows School. This in turn has since closed, and the buildings are currently being converted into homes.

◄ **COMBPYNE**
The Church 1900 45261

The parish church of
St Mary the Virgin (centre)
with its lofty belfry tower
stands beside Granary
Cottage and Long House
(left) that were attached
to Manor Farm. These
buildings are said to be on
the site of a nunnery that
belonged to Newenham
Abbey, near Axminster. The
church, built in 1240, has a
medieval mural featuring a
ship. Harbour Close (centre
right) takes its name from
the village pond, which is
known, ironically, as the
Harbour. Pyne Cottage,
in Lidyates Lane (centre
background), is a reminder
of the ancient family who
owned the village, which
lies in the combe that
gave Combpyne the other
element of its name.

► **PINHAY** *1922* 72780

This mansion on Lyme's western cliffs,
a mile beyond Ware, was the far point
on Jane Austen's walk from Dorset into
Devon in 1804. She described herself as
'a desperate walker', but her eagerness
was constrained by the necessity to be
'fussy and correct' in ensuring that she
set off wearing the right attire. James,
the coachman, cleaned her shoes before
and after. The terrain must have offered
a walk on the wild side to a young lady
from the easy-going landscape of the
Hampshire Downs. John Ames, who
bought the coastal estate in the 1840s,
set about closing the ancient right of way.
The case against was fought by Joseph
Hayward of Silver Street through his
son, the barrister and essayist Abraham
Hayward (1801-84).

CANNINGTON VIADUCT
1903 50253

This view looks north-westwards from Horseman's Hill. Having curved from the woods on Shapwick Hill (top right) and around Combpyne Hill (centre), the new six-mile railway line from Axminster to Lyme Regis crossed the deep-cut valley at Cannington. The viaduct, supported on nine piers, is 609 feet long and 93 feet high. It remains a state-of-the-art example of concrete construction, though the third arch from the west had to be reinforced with a pair of inner arches. The engineer was Arthur Pain, and the contractors were Baldry & Yerburgh of Westminster, who imported materials via the Cobb at Lyme on the ketch 'Ida'. Despite the scale of the engineering, the cost of building the line, including land acquisition, was a reasonable £67,000.

The branch line opened on 24 August 1903 and closed on 29 November 1965.

LYME REGIS *from the air 1946* AFR7547

SEASCAPE

THE CLIFFS *1906* 54538

We are looking eastwards along gated Ware Lane (centre) to Golden Cap (skyline, centre right) and Lyme Bay (right). Lyme Regis is only a mile away, beyond the next bend, but lies hidden behind the woods at the Holm Bush and what is now National Trust land at Ware Cliffs (top left). Several fields, formerly part of Ramscombe Farm, were purchased in 1987. They extend down to Devonshire Head (centre right). The view is from Furze Close, beside the grounds of Ware House (to the left).

THE COBB *1922* 72778

This view looks southwards across Lyme Bay from the main path through Langmoor Gardens, which were given to the town by James Moly of Langmoor Manor, Charmouth. The path emerges in Pound Street. The project to create the gardens was undertaken by borough surveyor Frederick Hugh McDonnell, and the elegant gates at Top o' Town were ceremonially opened by the Mayor, Henry Octavius Bickley, in June 1913. The medieval Cobb harbour spreads out below (centre left) with a shingle beach separating it from Cobb hamlet (centre).

FROM THE WEST *1890* 27344

From Ware Cliffs we can see the medieval Cobb harbour (centre right) and the coastal skyline of Stonebarrow Hill, Golden Cap and Thorncombe Beacon. St Michael's Church can be glimpsed in Lyme Regis town, below the Spittles and Black Ven (top left). The interesting buildings with a smoking chimney comprise the cement works (lower right). Behind this stacks of bricks surrounding the brick kiln stretch towards Ozone Terrace (centre). The shingle expanse of Monmouth Beach extends seawards. The factory site became a Royal Air Force base for operating air-sea rescue craft and bombing range launches during the Second World War.

THE HARBOUR *1890* 27361

This view looks seawards across Cobb hamlet. Its buildings range from Bay Cottage (near left), the Royal Standard, Sunnyholme, the Bonded Store, and the Coastguard Station to the old Cobb Arms (right). Bay Cottage had a fictional resident, Caption Harville, in Jane Austen's 'Persuasion'. The real-life landlord at the Cobb Arms was Jonathan Abbott. The picture is from the terraced Tennis Grounds; by Victorian times these were the town's main exercise area, after bowling fell out of favour and golf courses had yet to be constructed. The North Wall of the harbour (left centre) was still detached from the beach. The coaster 'Glencoe', which can be seen beside the Cobb Warehouse (centre), generally delivered coal and left with a cargo of Lyme-made cement.

THE HARBOUR FROM COBB ROAD
1890 27359

Cobb Road, as we see it today, dates from about 1830. Its narrow predecessor was described as a 'private road' in 1813. On the town's tithe map of 1841 it appears in its present width as 'New Road'. The view is southwards to the Cobb warehouses and Cobb hamlet (left), beyond Westfield (centre) and a terrace of early 19th-century town houses. No 6 (second from right) was the home of Captain Sir Richard Spencer (1779-1829), who experimented at the Cobb with self-buoyancy tanks for lifeboats in 1825, before sailing across the world to found the settlement of Albany in Western Australia.

THE COBB *1906* 54528

The Tennis Ground (near left) and the Royal Standard (left) are prominent; the Bonded Store of His Majesty's Custom and Excise was the biggest building (centre right). It is high tide in the harbour, where two sailing ships are berthed beside the Cobb Warehouses (centre). One of the premier ports of England in the Middle Ages, Lyme had long been declining in importance, though it was still important enough to be rebuilt in Portland stone after devastating damage in the Great Storm of 23 November 1824. Captain George Fanshawe of the Royal Engineers created the present smooth curves and water-dynamic sloping surfaces in 1825-26.

HARBOURSIDE

THE COBB *1900* 45239

This is the High Wall of the harbour, with Higher Walk on top and Lower Walk below, with the Gin Shop alcove and steps (left). This was named for a crane when it was the magazine for a gun battery. The picture, at low tide, looks northwards to Ozone Terrace, the Lifeboat Station (centre), the Coastguard Station and the Bonded Store, and along to the end of Cobb hamlet at Cobb Cliff (centre right). The houses above are West Cliffs, Holme Lea and Holm Craig (middle distance). Skyline rooftops extend from High Cliff (top left) to Coram Tower, Belmont, Buena Vista, Farnham and Poulett House.

THE COBB *c1955* L121220

We are looking eastwards from the Gin Shop at high tide to the Cobb entrance between the North Wall (centre left) and Cobb Warehouses (right). These date from before 1723. The view across the water is to the cliffs of Cain's Folly (left) and the skyline of Stonebarrow Hill, Chardown Hill and Golden Cap. This, at 617 feet above sea level, is the highest point on the south coast. All the coastline, comprising most of the parish of Stanton St Gabriel, was acquired by the National Trust between 1967 and 1972.

THE HARBOUR *c1955* L121116

Across the inner basin from the quay (right) beside the Cobb Warehouses is the 17th-century North Wall (centre), which protects the harbour from easterly gales. Beyond are Langmoor Gardens and the Bay Private Hotel on Marine Parade. The wooded skyline above the town extends from Rhode Barton and Thistle Hill to Penn Hill and Timber Hill. Vessels in the harbour range from fishing and pleasure boats registered at Weymouth (WH) and Exeter (E) to RAF launch No 1530 (top left). This, and the smaller No 363, were based at Lyme for bombing-range patrols and air-sea rescue purposes.

◄ **THE HARBOUR**
1892 31308

We are looking north-eastwards from the Lower Walk, across mooring lines in the sand, at low water; sailing vessels are moored beside the Cobb Warehouses (right). Beyond North Wall (centre) the panorama of the town includes Marine Parade, St Michael's Church and Church Cliff. Timber Hill forms the skyline.

28

THE HARBOUR
1925 76730D

South-westwards from the North Wall (left), across the harbour basin just about as empty as it would be today, are the Cobb Warehouses (centre) and Granny's Teeth steps, to the left of the couple who are standing on the High Wall which stretches out into Lyme Bay.

THE END OF THE COBB
c1910 L121301

That Meryl Streep moment, as it became after 'The French Lieutenant's Woman' had been filmed here in 1980, with the Outer Breakwater of the Cobb awash in a bursting south-westerly wave. The view is eastwards to Stonebarrow Hill and Cain's Folly (top left) and the familiar profile of Golden Cap (central skyline) with Thorncombe Beacon to the east (right). A fishing boat is venturing out from the Cobb, but no one has braved the slanting seat (which has since been removed). Frith's photographer, standing on the High Wall, must have been soaked.

GRANNY'S TEETH *1912* 65041

The ancient steps known as Granny's Teeth protrude from the inner side of the only surviving section of rough locally-sourced medieval walling at the Cobb. They were either left intact or re-set when Captain George Fanshawe of the Royal Engineers rebuilt all the other walls of the Cobb with smooth Portland stone in 1825-26. It was here, in Jane Austen's 'Persuasion', that Louisa Musgrove fell. The poet Alfred Tennyson walked across the hills from Bridport in order to see the spot in August 1867.

VICTORIA PIER *1912* 65043

Cousens & Company's paddle steamer 'Victoria' arrives from Weymouth. Victoria Pier used to be known as Crab Head until it was renamed following a visit by Princess Victoria with her mother the Duchess of Kent. On 31 July 1833, the royal yacht 'Emerald' was towed into Lyme by the steam packet HMS 'Messenger' to meet the royal party. They were escorted over the hills by the Earl of Ilchester's Yeomanry after spending a couple of nights at Melbury House. The Duchess and Princess were met at the Cobb on 2 August 1833 by the Mayor, John Hussey, and passed through a double file of coastguards. Then a floating platform and barge took the party and their carriages out to the 'Emerald'. The vessels weighed anchor at three o'clock and set off for Plymouth. This view is north-eastwards to Black Ven (top left), Charmouth and Cain's Folly (centre right).

VICTORIA PIER AND THE 'DUCHESS OF DEVONSHIRE' *1912* 65045

This low tide view from the Outer Breakwater looks northwards to Victoria Pier and the town as the Weymouth paddle-steamer 'Duchess of Devonshire' reverses away from the Cobb. The cobbler and town crier George Legg, in Silver Street, used to be the agent for the steamer operators Cosens & Company. Summer day trips reached beaches, piers and ports from Torquay to Bournemouth. This shot looks northwards to Marine Parade (centre) and beached boats at Cobb Gate.

THE HARBOUR
1925 76730B

We are looking from the Cobb Warehouses to the Coastguard Station and Old Bonded Store (centre); this was before the approach to the Cobb was transformed in 1937 with the building of the new Cobb Arms. Ozone Terrace is still partly visible (left),and so are weather-boarded Wings and Cobb Gate (centre right) behind the North Wall of the harbour. Cliffside buildings (centre background) include West Cliffs, Holme Lea and Holme Craig, but only High Cliff peeks out through the trees from above.

THE HARBOUR BEACH *c1965* L121263

Pebbles and sand extend below the Royal Standard; we look eastwards from deck-chairs, boats and canvas shelters to the North Wall of the harbour and the coast from Charmouth and Stonebarrow Hill to Golden Cap and Thorncombe Beacon.

◢ THE BEACH AND THE HARBOUR
c1955 L121193

There is safe bathing for children at high tide, protected from the open sea and its waves, behind the North Wall of the harbour. The shot is southwards from Bay Cottage and the Royal Standard to the Cobb Warehouses (centre right). Lyme was at its busiest in the mid 1950s, as post-war austerity eased, and before airliners opened up new horizons and brought foreign holidays within reach of the masses.

◂ *detail of* L121193

LYME REGIS *from the air 1946* AFR7547C

MARINE PARADE

GENERAL VIEW *1925* 76731

We view the town from the beach below the Royal Standard. The North Wall (right centre) has since been joined to the mainland (in 1979) by a random wall of rough boulders. Marine Parade (left centre) stretches beside the Bay Private Hotel and Madeira Cottage (centre) to Cobb Gate. Gun Cliff and Church Cliffs complete the town's seascape. Timber Hill rises above.

MARINE PARADE
c1955 L121202

Parasols and tables surround the Alice in Wonderland Tea Rooms. This stood on a terrace, below the site of a house called Wings, between Cobb Cliff and Bay Cottage, which as Jane's Café provided the closest competition. Beach trays were provided. North-eastwards is the Bay Private Hotel and Cobb Gate, with Gun Cliff beyond (right) and Timber Hill above (right top).

THE PARADE *1912* 65035

This shows the view from the Cobb hamlet to the original eastern cube-like core of the Bay Private Hotel (centre). Beyond are Madeira Cottage and the Assembly Rooms (centre right). The offshore rocks are Lucy's Ledge Jetty, Cobb Gate Jetty and Broad Ledge. Beach facilities comprise clusters of bathing tents and unfolded wood and canvas deckchairs.

37

▶ THE PARADE
1925 76730

Here we see landslipped Langmoor Gardens (left) before the building of retaining walls and amusement arcades. Telegraph poles carry the wires from Cobb hamlet to the town, which begins at the Bay Private Hotel (centre). This picture clearly shows the split-level look of the Walk, as it was known until Edwardian times, with the Cart Road being the lower terrace from Cobb Gate to the sands beside the Cobb. They have yet to be joined. The Cart Road was widened after severe storm damage in February and September 1974. The high sea wall dates from 1880.

LANGMOOR GARDENS AND THE PUTTING GREEN
c1955 L121211

We look north-eastwards, above the gable-end of the Bay Private Hotel (centre right), to the Spittles and Black Ven. Beyond are Charmouth and Stonebarrow Hill (top right). After being given to the town in 1913 by James Moly (and named for his home, Langmoor Manor, in the woods above Charmouth), Langmoor Gardens had a chequered career. By 1962 they were being torn apart by landslips, and the situation was much the same in 2005, with this area being sealed off.

▲ **MARINE PARADE** *1930* 83377

Cobb hamlet is sandwiched between Cobb harbour (left) and the somewhat landslipped Langmoor Gardens (right). The Old Bonded Store and Bay Cottage (centre) can be clearly seen. Bay Cottage is better known as Jane's Café, for its link with 'Persuasion'. Captain Wentworth brought the unconscious Louisa Musgrove here after her fall from Granny's Teeth on the Cobb. The closest buildings are Cobb Cliff and Wings (centre right) - Wings stood from 1827 to 1945. Though it looked ancient, it was not standing in Jane Austen's time, and therefore could not have been her lodgings, as was supposed. Its poetically magical name was the inspired creation of Mrs Culthorpe on moving into the house. 'I am surrounded by seagulls,' she used to tell people.

THE BEACH *1930* 83379

This photograph shows Marine Parade and its beach-tents, between Langmoor Gardens (top left) and the 1922-built Bay Private Hotel (centre). The remainder of Lyme's seafront continues to Cobb Gate and Church Cliffs (right). This spot, and Lyme generally, was obviously favoured by families with young children. The town's population, at the 1931 census, was only 2,620. It was estimated to double in summer, and more than triple during peak times, such as bank holidays and school holidays.

▼ **MARINE PARADE** *1930* 83373

Beyond the Bay Private Hotel and Madeira Cottages (left centre) are Hardown Hill, Stonebarrow Hill (centre) and Golden Cap (right). Seaward are a series of ledges. Lucy's Ledge Jetty (lower right) was constructed by the eminent geologist Sir Henry de la Beche in 1820. Cobb Gate Jetty, Long Ledge and Broad Ledge lie below the ancient heart of the town (centre right). Beach-tents line the Cart Road, and pedestrians use the Walk as a promenade (centre foreground).

► **FROM THE BEACH**
1907 58089

The four-storey Sundial Cottage (left), and Library Cottage next door are shown before the building of the Bay Private Hotel. The view is north-eastwards along Marine Parade, to Madeira Cottages, Pyne House and the Assembly Rooms, with the cliffs of Cain's Folly in the distance (far right). Offshore, low water has exposed the length of Lucy's Ledge Jetty (centre) and Cobb Gate Jetty beyond (right).

◄ **LOW TIDE**
1930 83381

An incredibly low ebb-tide, which would also have coincided with one of the highest tides of the century, has exposed the rock pools on Lucy's Ledge. Far above is Lucy's Ledge Jetty (centre), which was the creation in 1820 of pioneer geologist Henry de la Beche, who grew up in the town. Double rows of beach tents (centre left) line the Cart Road to the south of the Bay Private Hotel. The picture shows the view north-westwards to Langmoor Gardens (top left). Sundial Cottage and Library Cottage (centre right) look out across Marine Parade.

► **THE PARADE AND THE BEACH** *1922* 72762

We look north-westwards at low tide to the cuboid shape of Sundial Cottage, and Library Cottage, which incorporates exotic but re-set older lead-work from France. It takes its name from having housed a bookshop, which traded as the Marine Circulating Library in 1840. The architect and artist Arnold Mitchell retired here. He designed nearby Sundial Cottage in 1903 in Arts and Crafts style, incorporating ammonites and dinosaur parts. The thatched Madeira Cottages (centre) were built in 1818. Eminent visitors staying there included the cartoonist George Cruikshank, the author Captain Frederick Marryat, and the poet Walter de la Mare. Its four dwellings are Benwick Cottage, Harville Cottage, Madeira Cottage and Little Madeira. Next is No 6 (centre right), with balustrades, cast-iron fittings, storm protectors and honeycomb-style wall cladding of hexagonal slates.

MARINE PARADE

1925 76730E

We can see from the Bay Private Hotel along to Benwick Cottage and Harville Cottage (right) at Madeira Cottages. Between them are the solid shapes of Sundial Cottage and Library Cottage, and No 11 with its gabled frontage above an arched doorway (centre right). The ladies beneath the umbrella are heading south-west towards Langmoor Gardens, Cobb Cliff and Wings, in Cobb hamlet (far left). Behind these distant buildings stand the twin chimneys of the cement works.

THE PARADE FROM THE EAST *1907* 58091

We are looking from Cobb Gate Jetty beside the Assembly Rooms (far right). The buildings (right) include the Alcove Hotel, semi-detached Sunnybank, Library Cottage and Sundial Cottage (centre). Beyond the boats and boatmen the old Cart Road to the Cobb harbour passes above Lucy's Ledge Jetty (centre left) and then below Cobb Cliff and Wings (top left).

MARINE PARADE *c1955* L121243

Frith's photographer originally titled this as 'The Walk', which was the old Lyme name for the upper length of Marine Parade long into the 20th century. A plaque records that it was the inspired idea of the Corscombe libertarian philanthropist Thomas Hollis (1720-74) in 1771. He also endowed Harvard University's library. The familiar K6 telephone kiosk (left), a 1930 design by architect Sir Giles Gilbert Scott, adds a misleading touch of continuity. Just a decade before, fortified lookouts and pillboxes guarded this scene, and a mass of girders and wires bristled above a mined beach. By 1955 The Bay Private Hotel (centre) is catering again for civilians. The distant view is north-eastwards to Cain's Folly and Stonebarrow Hill, above Charmouth.

THE PROMENADE
c1955 L121244

Marine Parade is bustling. To the left is the lower entrance to Langmoor Gardens, with a memorial clock (top left) to those associated with the town who lost their lives in the Second World War. Then come the Bay Private Hotel (centre), Pyne House and the Alcove Hotel, and a glimpse of Cain's Folly cliffs beyond Charmouth (top right). Fashions include shorts and open-neck nylon shirts. It was an age when a cyclist respected the rights of pedestrians by walking with his bicycle - though he looks a little incongruous with a coal-scuttle in his other hand.

EASTERN SEABOARD

THE PROMENADE *c1955* L121187

We are looking eastwards along the historic Cart Road from the Cobb, with an open-topped Austin to centre left. Behind are a line of cars parked at Cobb Gate, from which Cobb Gate Jetty stretches seawards (right). Signs advertise 'A Grand Trip to Beer' on the Devon coast and a 'Mackerel Fishing Trip Round the Bay' for two shillings. Marine Parade rises above (left), and in the distance are Cain's Folly, Golden Cap and Thorncombe Beacon.

▶ **OLD WALLS**
1922 72767

Cobb Gate Jetty is in the foreground, dating in its present state from 1850; it is on the site of Lyme's first early medieval harbour, which was washed away on 11 November 1377 with the loss of 77 houses. The view is northwards to the Old Boathouse in the Square, and the Assembly Rooms beside Bell Cliff at the bottom of Broad Street, which were pulled down in 1928. Other buildings include the Rock Point Inn (centre) and the Guildhall. Coastal features are the Buddle estuary of the River Lim (centre right) and Gun Cliff beyond, where the town's battery was positioned.

THE BAY
c1955 L121169

The Square and Cobb Gate at the seaward end of Broad Street, eastwards from Bell Cliff, with the line-up of parked cars including Rileys, a Hornet soft-top, Jowett, Standard and Austins. Tobacconist and confectioner R Keeley (left) is trading as the Car Park Shop. Jutting out at low tide are Gun Cliff Jetty, Long Ledge (right centre) and Broad Ledge. Beyond are the cliffs and skyline of Cain's Folly, Stonebarrow Hill, Langdon Hill and Golden Cap.

▲ **THE OLD SEA WALLS** *c1960* L121224

This is a historic lost view of Lyme's eastern cliffs before they were entombed and extended in 1984, by sea defence works which incorporated and hid sewage disposal facilities. The Buddle estuary was tucked between high walls (left centre), dating from about 1750, below the cupola of the Victorian Guildhall. Higher terraces held a battery at Gun Cliff (right centre), above which looms the modern lines of the Marine Theatre. Eastwards are Long Ledge, Curtis Cove and Broad Ledge, with Stonebarrow Hill in the distance.

GUN CLIFF AND COBB GATE FROM BACK BEACH *1890* 27362

Back Beach was the fiefdom of William Curtis & Sons, boatmen and fish merchants from nearby Long Entry on Church Cliffs. The spot was locally known as Curtis Cove. Long Ledge juts out behind in this view south-westwards to the Assembly Rooms and Marine Parade (centre). Beyond are Wings, Ware Cliffs and the Cobb (far left). Gun Cliff with the Drill Hall and the Guildhall dominate the immediate setting (upper right).

THE BUDDLE BRIDGE *1900* 45249

Here we see the 13th-century Buddle Bridge (centre) and the buildings of Bridge Street which crossed it until demolitions for road widening in 1913. Bridge Street was known as Beaufront Street until the Middle Ages, and the land still sloped down to the sea until these sea walls were built after the Civil War. The word Buddle, the ancient dialect name for the estuary of the River Lim, described its previous state as an outlet choked by shingle.

THE CHURCH, *The Interior 1900*
45248

A Victorian marble font, and a Norman arch set in the Anglo-Saxon walls of the tower, are positioned at the heart of what was originally designed as a cruciform church. The parish church of St Michael the Archangel, its earliest walls dating from about AD 980, has been much extended to the east (foreground). This view looks westwards from the present nave, which was widened and lengthened in 1505, through the arch into the earlier building. The chained bible (right) is a Breeches Bible published in 1560 (so called because in it, Adam and Eve were said to have made themselves 'breeches' rather than 'aprons' of fig leaves). The wall behind now has a brass plate to a soldier of the First World War, 22-year-old Cecil Clifford Sanders, who died in France on 22 July 1916.

THE CHURCH *1890* 27373

This is the east end of the chancel and side chapels of the parish church of St Michael the Archangel. These walls date from 1505, but the building becomes older as it rises to the west. The original church, dating back to Anglo-Saxon times, was cruciform in plan. The tower was thought to date from the 12th century, but repairs in the winter of 1994 revealed a much earlier window, dating from about AD 980, in the south wall of the ringing chamber on the second storey. This was blocked in 1210, and so was an arcade in the north wall of the western old nave, which is now the porch. Outside, the gravestone of the famous fossil hunter Mary Anning (1799-1847) and her brother Joseph is on the north side of the present nave (towards top right). Silver Street lives up to its medieval Latin name - 'silva', meaning a wood - as it rises through trees on the western skyline (top left).

STREET SCENES

THE OLD FOSSIL SHOP
c1891 L121417

The Victorian Fossil Depot was first run by James Dollin. He was followed by Thomas Seager, who may well be the gentleman smoking a pipe (centre left). The sign between the upper windows boasts that the shop was patronised by HRH Prince Alfred, Duke of Edinburgh (1844-1900), the second son of Queen Victoria, who died before his mother. Then, as now, dinosaur bones and ammonites were the mainstay of Lyme's fossil trade. The Fossil Depot was demolished in 1913, when the last owner was Sidney Curtis, known as Dick - he died in 1928. The picture is eastwards from the Square into Bridge Street (left), where Obadiah Bird was the grocer.

BRIDGE STREET *1909* 61625

The Pilot Boat Hotel (left) is pictured in the time of Robert Warren, advertising livery stables, carriages and transport for invalids, as well as daily coaches to and from Bridport, which was the closest rail link until the Edwardian era. This remarkable photograph, looking north-eastwards along Bridge Street, shows weather-boarded buildings on the ancient Buddle Bridge. These, and the Fossil Depot (right), were demolished for a road-widening project in 1913. In the process it revealed Norman arches and probable remains of a chapel, as well as the underground room of a hermit, who was probably attached to Sherborne Abbey. Taxes and tolls for salt production may have been exacted at this point on behalf of the Abbot of Sherborne.

LYM BRIDGE ANTIQUE SHOP *c1955* L121241

We are looking eastwards along Bridge Street to the Buddle Bridge (centre right) over the River Lim. Lym Bridge Antique Shop (right) and A Daniels & Son, a fishmonger's, are across the water from two grocers' shops. Bragg's Stores (centre) face competition from F and L E Foxwell (left), where a Corona lorry, loaded with crates of soft drinks, is delivering. Guildhall House is the white-fronted building on the corner (far centre).

▼ **BRIDGE STREET** *c1965* L121270

The shop-front of F and R Younger (left), previously the grocer's P and L E Foxwell, and before that Brown's High Class Stores, which was established in 1812, stands opposite the Philpot Museum (right). We are looking eastwards along Bridge Street to the Guildhall (centre) and Guildhall Cottage (centre left).

▶ **THE MUSEUM**
1907 58100

Designed by architect George Vialls for the Mayor, Thomas Embray Davenport Philpot, the museum in Bridge Street was built in 1901. Its core collection, gathered together by Philpot's sisters at their home in Silver Street, was moved down the hill in stages, but the Philpot Museum did not open to the general public until 1921. Its curators have included local historians Cyril Wanklyn and Henry Chessell and the internationally acclaimed author John Fowles, who made his home at Underdown Farm and then moved into town, to Belmont. The shot is seawards (centre), through the arches, from the Guildhall (left).

◄ THE LYNCH
1892 31311

The Lynch Walk runs between the deep main channel of the River Lim (left) and the higher-level leat towards Town Mills (right). These used to be known as King's Mill, and royal consent was given for the construction of this mill leat in 1341. The view is northwards to the Angel Inn (centre), still with its thatched roof, and Weaver's Cottage (centre right). The buildings on the other side of the river are Waterside (left) and Christopher's Cottage in Sherborne Lane (centre left).

► THE MILL
1892 31315

Corn-grinding Higher Mill (towards top left), which also produced oil, is glimpsed through the trees above a waterfall on the River Lim. Higher Mill stood midway between Jericho (centre) and Horn Bridge. Biblical names here preserve the memory of Baptist squatters, who met here from 1653, and built a series of thatched hovels. The second cottage, known as Jordan (centre left), took its name from the point chosen for baptisms in what they called the Jordan River. Across the water, towards Slopes Farm, the fields were regarded as Paradise.

SHERBORNE LANE
1907 58099

This ancient packhorse route, inland from salt-making pans and the Cobb landing place, is named for Sherborne Abbey, which owned Lyme's seaboard enterprises from Anglo-Saxon times. The bay-windowed cottages (right) include Janaul, Foxall and Mayflower Cottage. Opposite are Apple Tree Cottage (far left) and Providence Place, followed by Sandpiper, Little Tern and April Cottage (centre), with the latter still thatched. Holly Cottage and Ivy Cottage are in the corner. The picture is north-eastwards to the gable ends of the Cedars and Garston (centre right).

SHERBORNE LANE *c1955* L121183

The north-eastern end of Sherborne Lane descends to Lym House and the Angel Inn (centre left). The walls of Garston, Waverley and Monks Way (left) face Chapel Cottage, which dates from 1780 and has a fashionable frontage of Ionic pilasters and a pediment. Bed and Breakfast is on offer in this picture, which also shows the end wall of Cobblestones (right) and gable-end of Sea Horses.

SILVER STREET *1906* 54530

Appropriately still running beside trees at Burley Villas and Abbeyfield (centre), Silver Street was named in the Middle Ages for the Latin word for a wooded setting, rather than the precious metal. Today there are woods for much of the way to Uplyme and beyond. The three-storey Masons' Arms (left), where the landlord was George Hodder, has been replaced by a modern library set back from the road. Opposite, however, the scene is intact, including the front wall of the White House (right), the gable-end of the Lodge, and at a dental surgery behind. The view is north-westwards, up from Broadway House at Top of Town, along the main road out of town towards Hunter's Lodge, Axminster and Crewkerne.

▼ POUND STREET *1912* 65046

We look eastwards from the bushes and wall of The Grove (left). This large Victorian villa was destroyed by fire in 1952, which enabled widening of the street. Opposite are No 9 (right) and No 8, Shamien House, with No 6, St Anne's and No 5, Burton House being the next visible building. Between them is the entrance to No 7, St Michael's House. Finally, towards Top of Town, is Poulett Lodge (centre) beside the grounds of the Hotel Alexandra.

▶ BROAD STREET *c1905* L121001

The view down the town's busiest trading place begins with grocer and wine merchant Sarah Chapman's shop front (left) facing the Volunteer Inn (far right), where the landlord was Tom Searle. Down the north side of the street are the post office, and the Great House, where William Pitt the Elder, Earl of Chatham brought his 15-year-old son, Pitt the Younger, to recover from illness in 1773. Down the other side are Dunster's Library, founded by Frederick Dunster; then comes Miss Wilson's ironmonger's, which carries a plaque recording that here, in Raymond House, 'a critical meeting of the Corporation of Lyme Regis was adjourned to this house owing to turbulence and riotous conduct in the Guildhall'.

◀ THE SMITHY
1909 61633A

Amid displaced stairs and other paraphernalia, Samuel Govier (1855-1934) shoes a horse at the forge in Broad Street, where in 1895 he had been immortalised by the American artist James Abbott McNeill Whistler (1834-1903) in his painting 'The Master Smith of Lyme Regis'. The painting was sold to a New York dealer, and purchased by Boston Museum. Established by George Govier, the forge became Watson's Garage, founded by Jack Watson, before being redeveloped as Woolworths.

▶ BROAD STREET
1930 83384

We are looking downhill from the post office (left) and Dunster's Library (right), where the proprietor was Sydney Mould. A poster for Southern National gives the bus times to Bridport, Chard and Seaton. Next-door, behind the parked Austin, was Miss Wilson's ironmonger's (centre right). Opposite are signs for a 'Day and Night Telephone' and the star-sign of the Star Tea Company (centre left), with the Royal Lion Hotel further down the street.

▶ **BROAD STREET**
1900 45243

The shop window at No 26, the draper Henry Octavius Bickley (right), contains clothing and parasols. The period facade and shop front next door of Lockes Library has since been completely redeveloped for the Midland (now HSBC) Bank. Beside it is the alleyway to Holmcroft. Further down the street are No 21 (formerly the Dorsetshire Bank), and the Three Cups Hotel (projecting, centre). Buildings opposite include No 52, Ye Olde Tobacco Shoppe, and what is now Turles Bistro uphill from the Royal Lion Hotel. The photographic angle is south-eastwards, down to Bell Street Stores (centre left), run by the grocer E J Coombes.

BROAD STREET *c1955* L121109

Historic association abound in this section of the main street. Ye Olde Tobacco Shoppe (left) was the home of blacksmith Samuel Govier, who provided the artist James Abbott McNeill Whistler with a back room for his studio. Aveline House, the Georgian building housing Lloyds TSB Bank on the site of Tower House, was the home of William Aveline. His distinguished geologist stepson, Sir Henry Thomas de la Beche, lived here as a teenager. Shop fronts include those of the Tudor Cafe, Eastmans, and The Nook. The Royal Lion Hotel and New Inn are followed by Middle Row (centre). The Toby Jug, Fudge Kitchen and Mulberry Manor front the next pavement, in a row of shops uphill to the Three Cups Hotel. Pyne House in all probability stands on the site of the lodging house where Jane Austen stayed. Albert Thomas Baker's garage was in the main street (right) with signs for restaurants on either side.

BROAD STREET
1909 61627

The three-storey Royal Lion Hotel (left) incorporates a Tudor building. King Edward VII, as Prince of Wales, spent a night here during a teenage walking tour in September 1856. As a result it gained royal cachet, and the Prince's emblem of feathers sprang from the parapet above the name of landlord Robert Lutke. From a bay window in 1895, Whistler the artist spotted a grocer's daughter Rose Rendall in the street, and decided to paint his 'Little Rose of Lyme'. As with Whistler's other major Broad Street portrait, it was bought by the Boston Museum. Down the street, the Assembly Rooms (centre) can be seen protruding from behind Middle Row. Holiday-related businesses include a Post Card Depot and a photographer's Kodak sign. Opposite the Royal Lion, until it moved up the street, was the post office (right).

▶ **BROAD STREET** *1900* 45242

We are looking north-westwards up Bell Street from the Assembly Rooms. Middle Row juts out (bottom left), and the raised pavement leads to Bell Cliff (bottom left). No 11, selling boots and shoes, together with Lipton's teas (left), was the shop of clothier Harry Lane. No 12 was another tailor, Sidney Wellman (centre left). Next-door, in Pyne House, above the shop of chemist Henry Matthew Neale at No 13, Miss Phyllis Sheppard taught music. Further up the hill is the bow-fronted Three Cups Hotel (centre). Opposite are the bay windows of Royal Lion Hotel and the flat frontage of the New Inn, where landlady Mrs Sarah Spencer was followed by William G Cornish. The blind belongs to the shop of watchmaker and jeweller James Wheller Farnham, and grocer George John Rendall traded from No 62 (bottom right). This was the home of Rose Rendall, whom Whistler painted.

BROAD STREET *c1955* L121198

The chemist's (left) became Holman, Ham & Company. Shop signs beyond the Three Cups Hotel include those of a Co-op store, the Tudor Cafe, and the Nook. Above the bay windows of the Royal Lion Hotel (right) the name of the former landlord Robert Lutke has been replaced by the motto of the Prince of Wales - 'Ich dien' - to go with his emblem of three feathers on the parapet. Captain Reginald R Slater was the publican during the Second World War, and Lionel Curtis was the landlord at the New Inn through the middle of the 20th century. Richards' Gifts (far right), at No 61, had a window of pewter, jewellery and watches.

▲ **THE SQUARE** *c1955* L121128

We are looking down on The Square from Middle Row at the bottom of Broad Street. The shot is north-eastwards, along Bridge Street (centre) to the roofs of Coombe Street. Hubert Charles Parham was the draper at No 64 Broad Street (bottom left). Between here and the Pilot Boat Inn, the public lavatories mark the site of the old Custom House, which was destroyed by fire in 1844. Along Bridge Street, behind a confusion of two-way traffic before installation of traffic lights, are the grocers P and L E Foxwell. The Rock Point Hotel carries the name of Exeter brewers Carr & Quick Limited, with a notice for the Vaults bar at the side (bottom right).

◀ *detail of* L121198

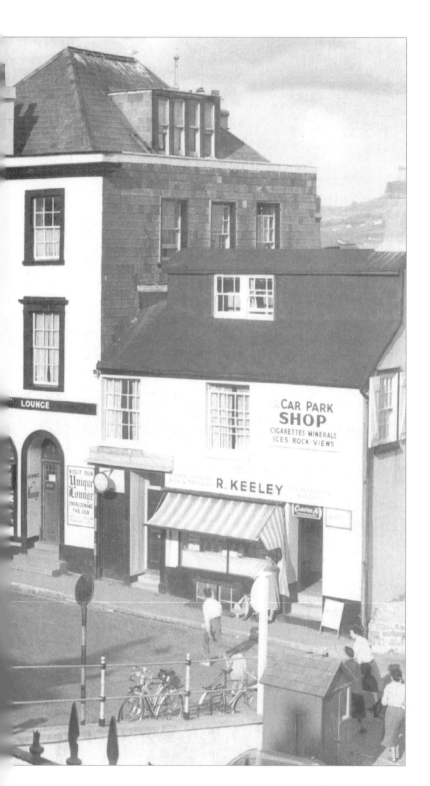

BROAD STREET

c1955 L121185

This view over The Square was taken from Bell Cliff. Second left is the Pilot Boat Inn, where the publican's dog, Lassie, licked back to life one of the sailors from the battleship HMS 'Formidable' on 1 January 1915. He had been pulled out of the sea after the ship had been torpedoed off Start Point with the loss of 600 men. Charles Atkins was the landlord. On the other side of Bridge Street are the Rock Point Inn (centre right), where steps and signs lead to its Town View Restaurant. R Keeley's Car Park Shop sells 'cigarettes, minerals, ices, rock, views'.

HOTELS, HOUSES AND SCHOOLS

THE HOTEL ALEXANDRA *1909* 61631

Poulett House in Pound Street was the home of dowager Lady Poulett during the Napoleonic Wars. It became the home of the Rev Edward Peek, of the wealthy Rousdon family, who converted the stable block into a chapel in 1884. As The Hotel Alexandra, owned by Archibald H Hinton, it claimed to be 'replete with every comfort in an old world town'. The elegant carriage has been tentatively identified as that of the Earl and Countess of Ilchester from Melbury House, which was shared by Lady Stavordale from Summer House, Evershot.

THE HOTEL ALEXANDRA *1906* 54533

This is the creeper-clad rear of the Hotel Alexandra, taken from its tennis lawn. The building faces the sea and the sun. Beside and behind the main building (right), facing Pound Street, is the Peek Memorial Chapel. After the conversion of Poulett House to the Hotel Alexandra, the owner Archibald H Hinton boasted that this was Lyme's 'only hotel in its own grounds'. In recent times it has been run by D J and Mrs N M Haskins.

◀ *detail of* 54533

THE PEEK MEMORIAL CHAPEL
The Reredos 1900 46049

The Rev Edward Peek, formerly the minister at Rousdon, retired to Lyme Regis, where he turned the stables of Poulett House into what became known as the Peek Memorial Chapel. He rebuilt it in English Renaissance style in 1884, with a High Church altar and an elaborate Venetian mosaic of Our Lord in Majesty. The building, which had seating for 80, is now the Poulett Hall.

▼ ST MICHAEL'S PRIVATE HOTEL
1925 76738

St Michael's House, the Victorian home of Mrs Brandham at No 7 Pound Street, became St Michael's Hotel. It was under 'entirely new management' in 1924, when the proprietors were Mr and Mrs Walter Hardy. We are looking south-eastwards from the carriageway; the next-door neighbours are St Anne's at No 6 (left) and Shamien House at No 8 (right). The building was empty and undergoing conversion and restoration in 2005.

▶ STILE HOUSE
1909 61630

Stile House is typical of the smarter villas of Regency Lyme. It takes its name from the adjacent Stile Path through the bushes (top left) from Pound Street to the Cobb. It was the home in Victorian times of Frank Morris. Then it became a hotel, trading as Stile House Pension, run by Ernest James Leeming. The picture looks westwards and shows semi-circular rooms with a flat roof at the north-east corner. Beyond are Buena Vista (right) and Belmont (top).

◀ **UMBRELLA COTTAGE**
1930 83386

This is the town's smallest and most distinctive building. Umbrella Cottage is a cottage ornée of about 1825, and stands on Sidmouth Road. Though since extended to the south-west (right), the original building is set around a central chimney, with polygonal walls, a thatched roof, and an elaborately embellished carved oak door. It contrasts in size with High Cliff on the opposite side of the road, which was the home of Joseph Lister, 1st Baron Lister of Lyme Regis, who pioneered antiseptic surgery.

CORAM COURT GUEST HOUSE *1930* 83385

Coram Court, named for the Lyme-born philanthropist Sir Thomas Coram, who founded the Hospital for Foundlings in Brunswick Square, stands beside Coram Tower (to the right). The view is northwards from Sidmouth Road. It was built as the Vicarage in 1851 and became the home of Sir John Arrow Kempe (1846-1928), who chaired the Board of Customs from 1894 and was then Comptroller and Auditor-General. After his death it was taken over by the Holiday Fellowship.

THE COLLEGE *1890* 27371

This is the rear of Coram Court – we are looking south-westwards from its grounds. It became St Michael's College in 1887, with the Rev Arthur R Sharpe as headmaster. There were 34 pupils initially, and the advertised aim was 'to provide a good education at moderate charges for the sons of the clergy of the dioceses of Salisbury and Exeter'.

SUMMER HILL *1909* 61629

Summer Hill House, on the west side of Charmouth Road, was the Victorian home of the borough magistrate Walter Banfield Wallis. Then the house became nationally known for the most liberal educational regime in the land. Summerhill School was founded here in 1924 by the child psychologist Alexander Sutherland Neill (1883-1973). As described in his autobiography 'Neill! Neill! Orange Peel!', it was a free school for the problem children of problem parents. The name went with it when Neill moved the school to Leiston, Suffolk. Meanwhile, at Lyme in 1930, Mrs T G Miles was the proprietress of Summerhill Private Hotel. It has since been greatly extended, with additional wings, and converted into prestigious apartments.

THE COTTAGE HOSPITAL *1906* 54531

This photograph shows the view north-westwards up Church Street from beside the Old Monmouth Hotel, with the churchyard railings on the right. The sign in front of the eight-bed Cottage Hospital (left) records that it was opened in 1897 as part of the town's commemoration of Queen Victoria's diamond jubilee. It moved in 1927 to be amalgamated with an earlier hospital in Pound Street. The house, now known as the Gables, looks much the same, apart from removal of the creepers and chimneys. Further up the street are the National Schools, dated 1892 (centre), behind the girl sitting on the steps.

THE VICTORIA HOTEL *1907* 58092

The Victoria Hotel stands in Uplyme Road, facing Clappentail
Lane (near right) from the corner with Roman Road (bottom left).
It was built in 1901, at the end of the longest reign on record.
William Worth Lloyd-Worth was the landlord until after the First
World War. F N Mantle was the publican during the Second
World War. The angle of the picture is south-eastwards, towards
the town, and may have been taken after a fire or some other
incident, judging by the number of interested bystanders.

THE SECONDARY SCHOOL *1925* 76742

Lyme's co-educational Secondary School for 125 pupils opened
in 1923. Its cabins were in keeping with the basic military hut-
like look of so many institutions built during the First World War
and afterwards. The school was in Hill Road, between Pound
Road and West Hill Road, with a view across the town, including
St Michael's Church (centre right), to Golden Cap (centre) on
the eastern seaboard of Lyme Bay. The headmaster, S L Watton
of Cranbrook in View Road, transferred to the new Lyme Regis
Grammar School - now the Woodroffe School - when it opened
above Uplyme Road in 1931.

UPLYME

UPLYME
The Mill c1900 U7301

This view of the northern extremity of the borough is from a meadow on the west side of the River Lim. On reaching the Old Mill, the footpath across the fields from Lyme becomes a double-hedged dirt track through a carpet of wild garlic into Uplyme village. 17th-century buildings and the wooden paddles of a mill-wheel are preserved in a thatched time-warp setting. There has been a corn mill on this site from Anglo-Saxon times, as part of a manor that belonged to Glastonbury Abbey.

UPLYME
Main Road c1965 U7008

This is the B3165, heading southwards to Lyme Regis, on the slope above Springhead. Mona House (left) was partly thatched until a fire in 1924, when Lady Jones was rescued from her bedroom window by the local publican climbing up a ladder. Behind is half-timbered Leacroft on Tapper's Hill (centre left). The arched windows on Tollgate Cottage (centre right) look out on what was a turnpike toll road. Beyond are Havering Cottage and Solways (top right). The road has since been widened at West End (right).

UPLYME, *Church Street c1960* U7011

We look eastwards down Church Street from the Main Road on the south side of the Talbot Arms and Doon Beg (far left). The windows on the left, open wide in the glorious hot summer, are at Myrtle Cottage and Penrith House. Across the road, beside the old-style 'Halt' sign, is Sunnybanks (right), where the corrugated iron roof has since been removed and replaced by thatch. Behind, towards trees beside the River Lim, are bungalows at Lymside and No 2.

▲ **UPLYME**
The Church 1900 46055

The parish church of St Peter and St Paul, a favourite dedication of King Ine in Anglo-Saxon times, stands on a knoll overlooking Uplyme village. The medieval church building was extensively restored in 1876, but the tower is much older. Graffiti on the bells from 1595 include an anchor and bishop's mitre. The clock on the tower dates from 1846. The picture is from the south, towards the ivy-clad frontage of Court Hall Farm (right).

◄ **UPLYME**
The Roost c1960
U7007

We are looking north-westwards up Spring Head Road from its junction with Mill Lane (foreground, right) and the bridge over the River Lim. Blossom Hill and Pound Lane are on the skyline (centre left). The house, known as the Roost (centre), is the home of the author Jack Thomas, whose novel 'Arnolfini: Reflections in a Mirror' is a tale of art detection.

UPLYME
Yawl Bottom 1900 45264

Though still standing between lone pines, the cottage known
as Snow Drop (centre right) now has a slate roof, and is the
Silverdale Sanctuary. The lean-to has been demolished.
Otherwise, apart from creeping suburbia, Yawl Hill Lane retains
its views over Yawl Bottom. This panoramic shot is south-
westwards, across the central part of Uplyme parish, to Ames'
Plantation on Woodhouse Hill (top right) and the coastal plateau
towards Rousdon.

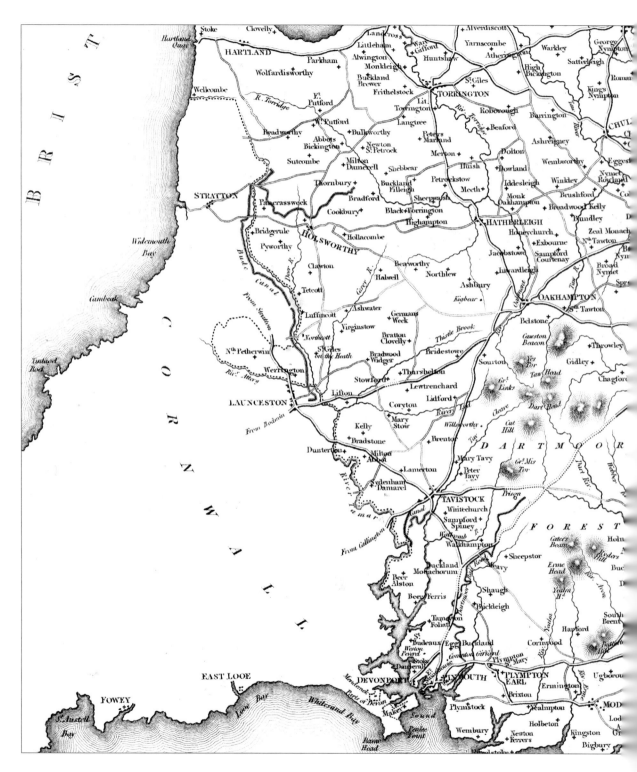

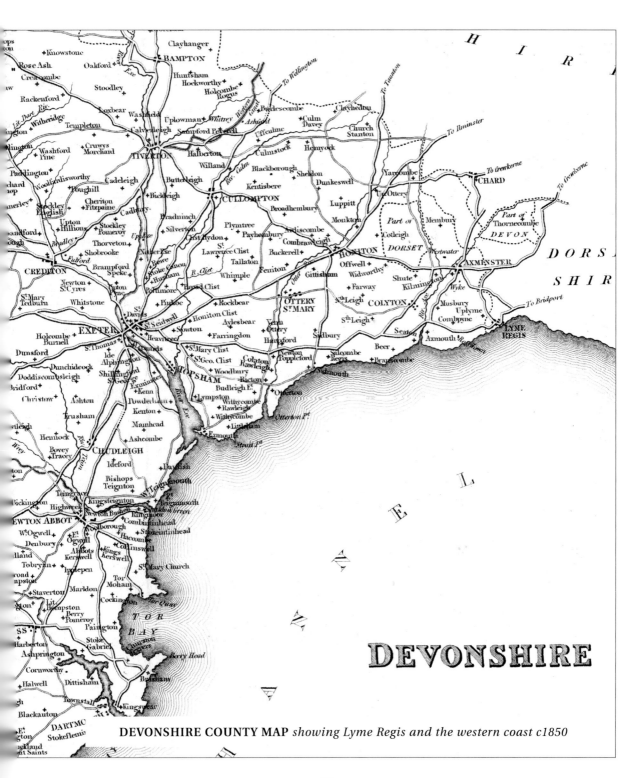

DEVONSHIRE COUNTY MAP *showing Lyme Regis and the western coast c1850*

CHARMOUTH

CHARMOUTH, *The Village 1890* 27381

We look north-westwards up The Street to the Coach and Horses Hotel (left centre), where the Victorian landlord was James Ingram. Charmouth House is further up the hill (centre). The shopkeeper Edward Archer Vince (centre right) ran the archetypal general store, and could claim to supply just about everything. The sign lists 'linen and woollens, clothing, hats, fancy articles, boots and shoes, groceries and ironmongery'.

CHARMOUTH, *High Street c1960* C66027

The turnpike road through Charmouth was run by the Bridport District Trust from 1764 to 1877. For several decades in the next century it carried the A35 Folkestone to Honiton trunk road. The lorry climbing the hill belonged to Grabham's Transport. This view is south-eastwards, towards Bridport, from Gear's Garage with its AA and RAC signs (far right). L M de Ville ran the Queen's Armes Private Hotel (right) in the mid 20th century, and Edward Hunter was across the street in the George Hotel (left). The early 16th-century Queen's Armes is described by the Royal Commission on Historical Monuments as 'an unusually complete example of a small late medieval house'. King Charles II spent a sleepless night here on 22 September 1651, disguised as a servant, during his escape from the Battle of Worcester to exile in France.

CHARMOUTH, *The Beach 1900* 46064

We are looking eastwards from the blocked mouth of the River Char, which ends its journey to the sea by having to break through a ridge of shingle (right). The coastal footpath from Charmouth (left) crosses to a shelter on Evan's Cliff (centre), but is then subject to recurrent problems as it crosses the landslip zone at Cain's Folly (central skyline). Here a Royal Air Force coastal radar station slipped down the cliffs on 14 May 1942. Its concrete and brick remains are entombed in the undercliff. The distant cliff, towards Bridport, is Thorncombe Beacon (towards top right).

CHARMOUTH
The Beach c1960
C66063

There are sea defences (top left) where Lower Sea Lane converges with Higher Sea Lane. Below, a shingle beach with patches of pea-grit provides a spot for rest and relaxation between Raffey's Ledge and the Mouth Rocks, where the River Char enters the sea. Evan's Cliff is to the east (centre), followed by the higher cliffs of Cain's Folly and Golden Cap (top right). Jane Austen writes in 'Persuasion': 'Charmouth with its high ground and extensive sweeps of country, and still more, its sweet retired bay, backed by dark cliffs where fragments of low rock among the sands make it the happiest spot for watching the flow of the tide; for sitting in unwearied contemplation.'

CHARMOUTH, *Rivermead Caravans c1960* C66086

These holiday caravans are sited behind Rivermead House. This was among the 'horror pictures' used by the land agent John Cripwell in order to encourage Lord Antrim and the council of the National Trust to buy two thousand of acres from Lyme Regis to Eype. Mobile homes between River Way and Bridge Road, on the west bank of the River Char, have also been targeted by nature, notably in a flash flood in the 1970s.

INDEX

NAMES OF SUBSCRIBERS

The following people have kindly supported this book by subscribing to copies before publication.

The Addiscott Family

Meg and Richard Alsopp

J H Barrow

James Beavis

Mr & Mrs D Booth

Bridport & Lyme Regis News

Janie Brown, Bridport

For William Camplin, my father from Lyme

Barry Clarke

H Collier

Mrs M Davey, Colyton

Keith and Sally Denman

With much love to my parents J S & J Dixon

For my son Jeffrey with love from Mum, Joyce Evemy

For my son Stephen with love from Mum, Joyce Evemy

James Everidge

Margaret Garrett, Lyme Regis

To Ruby Hanson, Fond memories of Lyme Regis, from Dilys

Alan & Vicki Herrick, Knowle & Lyme Regis

Mr Michael Hodder

To Mark Jones on his 50th Birthday

The Kavanagh Family, in memory of happy holidays

Jimmy and Jeanette Lemmon, Lyme Regis 2005

Doris Sylvia Loveridge

As a tribute to my parents, Mr & Mrs P F Marchant

Mrs Rosemary Norman

Mr & Mrs Oakley

Rosie Parham, Bradpole, Bridport

Peter, Susan & Ben Parker

Tony Payne & Family - Happy Memories of Lyme Regis

The Price Family, Coram Court, Lyme Regis

George P Pritchard

Janet Pulford, Witney

Rod & Bonny Robinson

Wendy & Frank Rogers of 'Thatch', Lyme Regis

Mr C F & Mrs J M Rowland, Taunton

The Royal Lion Hotel

Alan & Kathleen Saltmer, Charmouth

Michael Schofield & Family

Astra Seaton, Lyme Regis

Mrs Y Shortt, Lyme Regis

To Jack and Matthew Skinner - happy fossil hunting! love Mum

Tony & Reni Smith, Lyme Regis

The Squance Family, Lyme Regis

In memory of my husband, Stanley

In memory of winter walks along the Cobb, to Steve from Rosie

Helen Sweetland

Mr D J W & Mrs B E Taylor, Kilmington

Maxwell E Thorner

Miss P M Trounson

Doreen Tuck & Family, Lancelion, Western Australia

In memory of Auntie Flos from the Tuck Family of Christchurch

Kath Valler (nee Rattenbury), Lyme Regis

Mrs Dawn Vickers, Lyme Regis

Mrs D M Vickers, Lyme Regis

Brian A Whiscombe

Lewis Leonard Wicks, Seaton

To Mike and Billie Willcocks, to inspire more lovely paintings, love Julia

The Woodman Family

Mr Henry Woodward

The Worthing Family

FRITH PRODUCTS & SERVICES

Francis Frith would doubtless be pleased to know that the pioneering publishing venture he started in 1860 still continues today. Over a hundred and forty years later, The Francis Frith Collection continues in the same innovative tradition and is now one of the foremost publishers of vintage photographs in the world. Some of the current activities include:

Interior Decoration

Today Frith's photographs can be seen framed and as giant wall murals in thousands of pubs, restaurants, hotels, banks, retail stores and other public buildings throughout the country. In every case they enhance the unique local atmosphere of the places they depict and provide reminders of gentler days in an increasingly busy and frenetic world.

Product Promotions

Frith products are used by many major companies to promote the sales of their own products or to reinforce their own history and heritage. Frith promotions have been used by Hovis bread, Courage beers, Scots Porage Oats, Colman's mustard, Cadbury's foods, Mellow Birds coffee, Dunhill pipe tobacco, Guinness, and Bulmer's Cider.

Genealogy and Family History

As the interest in family history and roots grows world-wide, more and more people are turning to Frith's photographs of Great Britain for images of the towns, villages and streets where their ancestors lived; and, of course, photographs of the churches and chapels where their ancestors were christened, married and buried are an essential part of every genealogy tree and family album.

Frith Products

All Frith photographs are available Framed or just as Mounted Prints and Posters (size 23 x 16 inches). These may be ordered from the address below. From time to time other products - Address Books, Calendars, Table Mats, etc - are available.

The Internet

Already ninety thousand Frith photographs can be viewed and purchased on the internet through the Frith websites and a myriad of partner sites.

For more detailed information on Frith companies and products, look at these sites:

www.francisfrith.co.uk
www.francisfrith.com
(for North American visitors)

See the complete list of Frith Books at:

www.francisfrith.co.uk

This web site is regularly updated with the latest list of publications from The Francis Frith Collection. If you wish to buy books relating to another part of the country that your local bookshop does not stock, you may purchase on-line.

For further information, trade, or author enquiries please contact us at the address below:
The Francis Frith Collection, Frith's Barn, Teffont, Salisbury, Wiltshire, England SP3 5QP.
Tel: +44 (0)1722 716 376 Fax: +44 (0)1722 716 881 Email: sales@francisfrith.co.uk

See Frith books on the internet at www.francisfrith.co.uk

FREE PRINT OF YOUR CHOICE

Mounted Print
Overall size 14 x 11 inches (355 x 280mm)

Choose any Frith photograph in this book.
Simply complete the Voucher opposite and return it with your remittance for £2.25 (to cover postage and handling) and we will print the photograph of your choice in SEPIA (size 11 x 8 inches) and supply it in a cream mount with a burgundy rule line (overall size 14 x 11 inches).
Please note: photographs with a reference number starting with a "Z" are not Frith photographs and cannot be supplied under this offer.
Offer valid for delivery to one UK address only.

PLUS: **Order additional Mounted Prints at HALF PRICE - £7.49 each** (normally £14.99)
If you would like to order more Frith prints from this book, possibly as gifts for friends and family, you can buy them at half price (with no additional postage and handling costs).

PLUS: **Have your Mounted Prints framed**
For an extra £14.95 per print you can have your mounted print(s) framed in an elegant polished wood and gilt moulding, overall size 16 x 13 inches (no additional postage and handling required).

IMPORTANT!

These special prices are only available if you use this form to order . You must use the ORIGINAL VOUCHER on this page (no copies permitted). We can only despatch to one UK address. This offer cannot be combined with any other offer.

Send completed Voucher form to:
The Francis Frith Collection, Frith's Barn, Teffont, Salisbury, Wiltshire SP3 5QP

CHOOSE A PHOTOGRAPH FROM THIS BOOK

Voucher for **FREE** and Reduced Price *Frith Prints*

Please do not photocopy this voucher. Only the original is valid, so please fill it in, cut it out and return it to us with your order.

Picture ref no	Page no	Qty	Mounted @ £7.49	Framed + £14.95	Total Cost £
		1	Free of charge*	£	£
			£7.49	£	£
			£7.49	£	£
			£7.49	£	£
			£7.49	£	£
			£7.49	£	£
			* Post & handling		£2.25
			Total Order Cost		£

Please allow 28 days for delivery.
Offer available to one UK address only

Title of this book ....

I enclose a cheque/postal order for £ ....
made payable to 'The Francis Frith Collection'

OR please debit my Mastercard / Visa / Maestro / Amex card, details below

Card Number

Issue No (Maestro only)   Valid from (Maestro)

Expires   Signature

Name Mr/Mrs/Ms ....
Address ....
....
....
.... Postcode ....
Daytime Tel No ....
Email ....

ISBN 1-85937-956-6   Valid to 31/12/07

Would you like to find out more about Francis Frith?

We have recently recruited some entertaining speakers who are happy to visit local groups, clubs and societies to give an illustrated talk documenting Frith's travels and photographs. If you are a member of such a group and are interested in hosting a presentation, we would love to hear from you.

Our speakers bring with them a small selection of our local town and county books, together with sample prints. They are happy to take orders. A small proportion of the order value is donated to the group who have hosted the presentation. The talks are therefore an excellent way of fundraising for small groups and societies.

Can you help us with information about any of the Frith photographs in this book?

We are gradually compiling an historical record for each of the photographs in the Frith archive. It is always fascinating to find out the names of the people shown in the pictures, as well as insights into the shops, buildings and other features depicted.

If you recognize anyone in the photographs in this book, or if you have information not already included in the author's caption, do let us know. We would love to hear from you, and will try to publish it in future books or articles.

Our production team

Frith books are produced by a small dedicated team at offices in the converted Grade II listed 18th-century barn at Teffont near Salisbury, illustrated above. Most have worked with the Frith Collection for many years. All have in common one quality: they have a passion for the Frith Collection. The team is constantly expanding, but currently includes:

Paul Baron, Jason Buck, John Buck, Ruth Butler, Heather Crisp, David Davies, Louis du Mont, Isobel Hall, Lucy Hart, Julian Hight, Peter Horne, James Kinnear, Karen Kinnear, Tina Leary, Stuart Login, Sue Molloy, Glenda Morgan, Wayne Morgan, Sarah Roberts, Kate Rotondetto, Dean Scource, Eliza Sackett, Terence Sackett, Sandra Sampson, Adrian Sanders, Sandra Sanger, Julia Skinner, Miles Smith, Lewis Taylor, Shelley Tolcher, Lorraine Tuck, Miranda Tunniclisse, David Turner, Amanita Wainwright and Ricky Williams.